INSTANT
TENNIS
LESSONS

D0374641

INSTANT TENNIS LESSONS

By the Editors of Tennis Magazine
Illustrations by Jim McQueen and Ed Vebell

A Tennis Magazine Book

All rights reserved including the
right of reproduction in whole or
in part in any form
Copyright © 1978 by
Tennis Features, Inc.

Published by
Tennis Magazine
A New York Times Company
495 Westport Avenue
Norwalk, Connecticut 06856

Trade book distribution
by Simon and Schuster
A Division of Gulf & Western Corporation
New York, New York 10020

First Printing
ISBN: 0-914178-18-0
Library of Congress: 77-92905
Manufactured in the United States of America

INTRODUCTION

Would you like the opportunity to pick the minds of the best tennis teachers in the game for their key instruction pointers? Of course you would. What tennis player wouldn't?

That's what this book offers you. From the pages of TENNIS magazine, we've taken the finest of the tennis tips presented each month by a number of the nation's leading instructors—the members of the United States Professional Tennis Association (USPTA). And we've combined them into 84 instant lessons to give you a quick yet comprehensive program for improving your game—no matter what your level of play.

This series of private lessons from USPTA teaching professionals closely approximates the conditions of a real lesson. And like the instructor giving a lesson, this book actually instructs you in what to do. It isolates the key elements that are involved in hitting a tennis ball successfully, blending text and drawings so that you will remember each one once you've put the book down and face your opponent across the net.

Each of the instant lessons on the following pages has been reviewed and approved by the members of TENNIS magazine's Instruction Advisory Board—Tony Trabert, Vic Seixas, Ron Holmberg, Roy Emerson, George Lott, Bill Price and Margaret Court—all of whom are distinguished coaches as well as former leading players. The material was edited for the magazine by managing editor Jeffrey Bairstow and illustrated by two of the top sports artists in the business, Jim McQueen and Ed Vebell.

There are two ways for you to use this book most profitably. The first is to read through it and absorb its lessons stroke by stroke. The second is to keep it handy for those times when your game seems to need some remedial work; if you develop a problem with a particular stroke, you will almost certainly be able to pinpoint the reason by consulting these pages.

Instant Tennis Lessons won't make you a better player instantly, but we do hope that its quick and graphic pointers will help you enjoy the game more right away.

—*Shepherd Campbell*
Editor

CONTENTS

GRIP

IMAGINE A BIRD IN THE HAND

Many players have difficulty mastering one of tennis' basic fundamentals: the proper pressure to apply on the grip. They are apt to squeeze the racquet handle too hard, which tightens up the shoulder and forearm muscles and hampers the stroke.

If you experience this problem, one way to learn to relax is to imagine that the racquet in your hand is a live bird. You want to hold it firmly enough so that it won't escape but not so hard that you'll crush it. With this amount of pressure, the racquet isn't held so loosely that it slips out of the hand. Yet your shoulder and forearm are relaxed and your body weight can be applied to a flowing, forward swing.

—*Claudia Long*

CONSISTENCY IS IN YOUR GRASP

Having trouble in making consistent shots? Try a firmer grip. You can strengthen your fingers, hand and wrist by squeezing an old tennis ball several times a day, while you are watching television, riding the train or bus to work, or anytime you have a spare moment. A firm grip should help you achieve consistent shots and, at the same time, avoid a sore elbow. But, don't squeeze the racquet so tightly that the sap runs out of the bottom of the handle! —*William M. Summers*

READY

CRADLE THE RACQUET WHEN WAITING FOR THE BALL

As you wait for the ball, cradle the throat of your racquet with your free hand. That will help you maintain a proper ready position with the racquet out in front of you and its head chest high. Keep your thumb on top of the racquet and your first two fingers underneath. The racquet face should be perpendicular to the ground and the head aimed at your opponent. Your free hand will not only take some of the weight of the racquet off your playing hand, it will also help with rapid grip changes.   —*Ben Foster*

IN THE READY POSITION, IMAGINE THERE'S A BALL UNDER YOUR HEELS

The next time you position yourself at the net, stay on the balls of your feet by imagining that there's a tennis ball under each of your heels. Keep returning to this ready position after each volley, never allowing your heels to touch the ground. The imaginary tennis balls will give you the bounce that you should have as you move quickly at the net. Of course, you should never put an actual ball under your feet; that could cause you to trip. But do stay on the balls of your feet as though imaginary tennis balls were under your heels.

—*Steve Greenberg*

WAIT WITH YOUR WEIGHT FORWARD

When you are waiting for an opponent to make his shot, keep your weight forward by standing on the balls of your feet. That will enable you to move quickly in any direction without the added delay of getting your weight up and forward as you prepare to pursue the oncoming ball. If you always wait with your weight on the balls of your feet, you'll get to all balls sooner.

—*John A. Kraft Jr.*

21

GET READY WITH BOTH HANDS ON THE RACQUET

Driving an automobile with only one hand on the wheel is tiring and dangerous. Using only one hand to guide your racquet when preparing for a ground stroke is similarly tiring and inevitably leads to poor positioning of the body. Keep two hands on the "wheel" when you're in the ready position and, as the ball approaches, use your free hand to guide the racquet back. That will trigger an automatic turning of your shoulders and help give you the proper weight transfer.   —*Donna B. Jaquith*

FOREHAND

GET A FAST START

As soon as you see the ball leaving your opponent's racquet, start running to the general area where the ball is headed. Don't wait until the ball clears the net. You can be the master of your fate only if you and your racquet arrive on time. —*Paul S. Fein*

RUN WITH YOUR RACQUET BACK

How many times have you gone after a relatively easy return, reached the ball and then flubbed the shot? There are few things more frustrating on the court. Why does it happen?

Often, the problem is that you neglected to get your racquet back soon enough. Don't wait until you get to the ball to start your backswing. Run with your racquet back and you'll be ready for the stroke the moment you arrive in position. The time to start the backswing is when the ball leaves your opponent's racquet and you've decided to take the shot on your backhand or forehand. Then, be ready to start swinging your racquet forward at about the time the ball bounces.

Remember, it's the early backswing that gets the good return.

—*Vince Eldred*

TURN YOUR SHOULDERS FOR MORE POWER

If your ground strokes lack power, you may be hitting the ball without first turning your shoulders sideways to the net. As the ball approaches, you should rotate your body while you take your racquet back so that your shoulders are at a right angle to the net. Then, as you hit through the ball, open your shoulders by turning them parallel to the net. By doing that, you'll automatically transfer your weight forward and put more power into your shot. So rotate those shoulders and put more zip into your ground strokes.

—*Gaines Goodwin*

TRIM YOUR BACKSWING

Unlike a normal ground stroke, the service return doesn't require a big backswing. Aim for about half a normal backswing and then bring the racquet forward to meet the ball out in front of you. The follow-through may also be a little shorter than with a normal ground stroke. A good service return demands lots of concentration and practice, but start with a shorter backswing and remember to follow through.

—*Dave Kornreich*

STEP OUT AT ONE O'CLOCK

If you find yourself hitting the ball late and uncomfortably on your forehand drives, check the position of your front foot as you step to make the shot. You should be stepping out so that the foot is pointed at the one o'clock position. That will help make sure that you meet the ball early out in front of your body and will allow you to lean forward comfortably. If you're stepping out at the three o'clock position, you'll not only meet the ball late but your movements will feel cramped. Go for the one o'clock direction and you'll have a free and easy forehand. —*Dave Kozlowski*

MOVE FORWARD ON DEEP BALLS

Many weekend players back up on deep balls. As a result, they forget to take the racquet back early and they hit the shot with their weight going backward rather than forward into the stroke. When a ball is hit to you, get your racquet back first, turn sideways to get ready for the shot and then hit the ball with your weight moving forward. Don't waste time backing up; get your racquet back early and move forward into the shot.   —*Rick Tavolacci*

37

LET YOUR KNEES ACT AS SHOCK ABSORBERS

Some players, particularly beginners, rarely bend their knees when they hit a ground stroke. As a result, they develop high, looping shots that lack both power and direction. A good way to help correct this problem is to think of your knees as shock absorbers that take the impact of your forward weight transfer as you hit a backhand or a forehand. Step toward the ball and bend down so that your racquet head can hit directly through the ball. Allow your "shock absorbers" to push you up again only when you complete the hit and start the follow-through.

—*James E. Shakespeare*

KEEP YOUR HEAD DOWN TO KEEP YOUR SHOTS DOWN

The key to hitting solid ground strokes is to transfer your weight properly from your back foot to the ball of your front foot as you swing forward. To do that effectively, you've got to keep your head down. If you pull your head up and back as you hit, your weight will stay on your rear foot and you'll probably lift the racquet abruptly—sending the ball skyward instead of straight over the net. Keep your head down and you'll be surprised how much power goes into your shots as a result of the proper weight transfer.

—*Ben Foster*

USE YOUR BACK FOOT AS AN ANCHOR

If you often find that you are off balance as you hit your ground strokes, the problem may be that you're leaning forward too much on your front foot. You then have to bring your back foot around to maintain your balance. Try thinking of your back foot as an anchor which must stay in contact with the ground throughout your shot. That will prevent you from leaning too far into the shot. So anchor your back foot to the ground to keep your balance.

—*James E. Shakespeare*

43

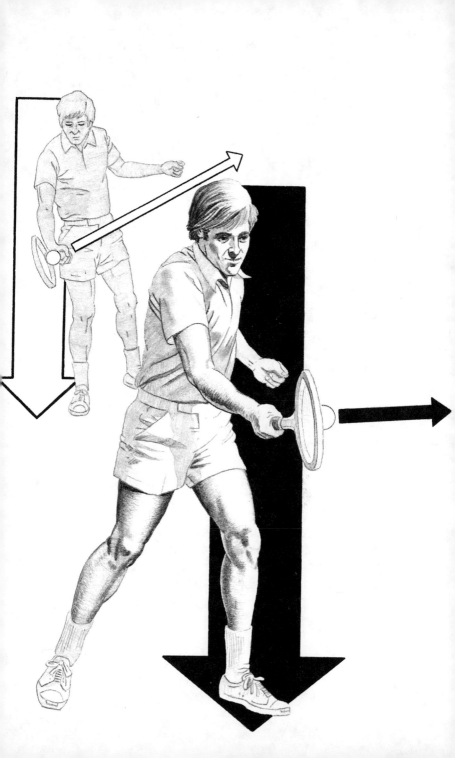

WATCH YOUR WEIGHT!

The most important single factor in hitting a tennis ball well is the distribution of your weight at the moment of impact. It should be on your front foot. That helps you in two ways: it gets more force into the ball and gives better control of the shot. On ground strokes, for instance, you should step into the ball with your weight well forward. If you don't, your weight will be on your back foot and the ball will tend to rise and lose force. So play the ball, don't let it play you. Get set quickly and swing through with your weight coming forward at the same time your racquet meets the ball.—*Hugh Curtler*

45

DON'T BE AFRAID OF A RISING BALL

Although it's usually best to hit the ball at the top of its bounce, there are some occasions when you will want to hit a rising ball. Go right ahead, but be sure to hit the ball with a racquet face that's vertical to the ground. Don't tilt the racquet back because you feel that's necessary to help the ball clear the net. All that will do is push the ball up high in the air and perhaps send it out of bounds.

Meet the ball as solidly as possible to neutralize any topspin that the ball may possess. Then hit through the ball with a vertical racquet face and a rising follow-through, and your shot will move crisply across the net.

—*John A. Kraft Jr.*

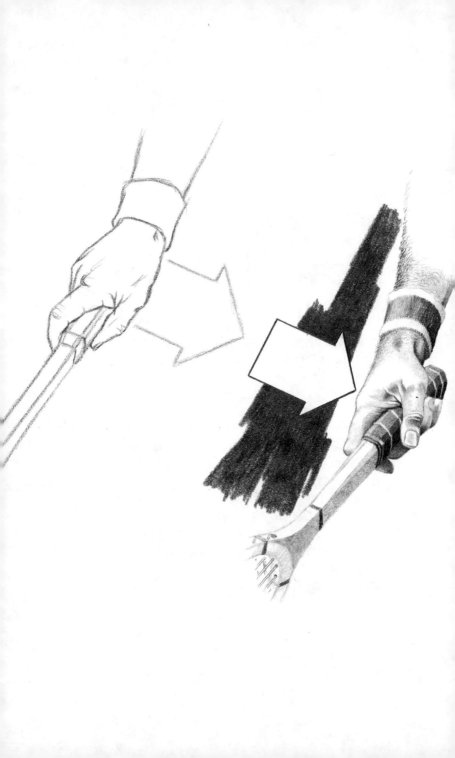

PUSH, DON'T PULL THE RACQUET

Just as it is always easier to push rather than pull a heavy object, it's easier to push a tennis ball through a stroke than it is to pull it. You can get your weight behind your racquet and push the ball if you use the proper Eastern forehand and backhand grips. That way, your wrist is always behind the racquet. And if you also remember to meet the ball out in front of your forward leg, you'll be stroking with less effort and more accuracy.

—Robert Givone

IMAGINE YOU'RE HITTING THE BALL WITH THE PALM OF YOUR HAND

If you're having trouble meeting the ball squarely on forehand drives, imagine that you are trying to hit it with the palm of your hand—almost as though you are playing handball rather than tennis. The palm would have to be held perpendicular to the ground for you to hit the ball properly. And that's the position your racquet should be in, too. If you have the feel of hitting through the ball with the flat of your hand, then you won't hit with a closed face, which will put the ball in the net, or with an open face, which will send the ball out of court. —*Don Allen*

HIT FLAT, DON'T SPOON THE BALL

When hitting ground strokes, do you find that your shots often sail up in the air? Chances are that you are "spooning" your strokes by allowing the racquet head to drop below the level of your wrist. The result is a scooping action which lifts the ball too far into the air. Remember to hit the ball with the racquet face at right angles to the ground. That way, you'll be hitting along the line of flight of the ball and your shots will go smoothly over the top of the net. Keep your racquet head up and you won't spoon your shots.

—*Peter Allen*

ON DEEP SHOTS, IMAGINE YOU'RE HITTING THROUGH 10 BALLS

To hit powerful and accurate ground strokes, you should keep the racquet on the ball as long as possible. One way to be sure you do that is to imagine that you are trying to contact each one of a line of 10 balls starting from a point opposite your front hip. Hit through the balls on a straight line and the result will be a powerful forehand or backhand which will send the ball deep into your opponent's court.

—*Ben Foster*

IRON OUT THAT FOLLOW THROUGH

Effective ground strokes demand a long follow-through for accurate control of the ball on your racquet. To extend your follow-through, imagine that your racquet is traversing a path along the top of an ironing board as you send the ball toward the other court. Try to hit through the ball, keeping racquet contact until your stroke reaches the end of the imaginary board. For each forehand stroke, point the tip of your ironing board in the direction you want to hit the ball and make sure that your follow-through continues in that direction.

—*Dave Woods*

FINISH WITH YOUR RACQUET HEAD AT HEAD LEVEL

When you are playing from the baseline, you need a long follow-through to make sure that your ground strokes land deep in your opponent's court. Follow through so that you complete your swing with your racquet roughly at the level of your head. This high finish will help you lift the ball so that it will clear the net by three or four feet and, thus, land deep in the opposing court. It will also help you put a little topspin on the ball. So remember to swing your racquet head up to head level as you follow through on ground strokes.   —Ben Foster

GET UNDER THE BALL AND OVER THE NET

Don't be afraid of hitting a ground stroke that makes the ball pass quite high over the net—perhaps as much as five feet. Hitting the ball higher will not only cut down on the chances of the ball going into the net, but will also send the ball deeper into the opponent's backcourt. For height, the forward swing must begin below the level where the ball is going to be hit. The follow-through should finish higher, usually above the player's head. Don't swing down on the ball or you'll be forced to pull up on the follow-through. Start low and finish high.

—John M. Brownlow

TARGET PRACTICE TO GROOVE YOUR FOREHAND

If you are just getting started in tennis, one of your first objects is to learn how to hit a forehand shot straight ahead. This target practice will help you. If you are right-handed, stand between positions B and C and hit against a backboard to target C. If you do it correctly, the ball will rebound to your forehand side. Don't attempt to alternate forehands and backhands against the backboard until you have fully grooved both strokes. —*The Editors*

BACKHAND

ON GROUND STROKES, HIDE YOUR RACQUET AS YOU PREPARE

When you prepare to hit a forehand or backhand drive, you should take your racquet back until it is almost completely hidden from your opponent. It should be pointing at the fence directly behind you so that the racquet, your body and your opponent are all in one line. If your opponent can see your racquet in front of your body when you have the racquet all the way back, your backswing is too short; if your opponent can see your racquet behind your back, your backswing is too long.

—*Ben Foster*

DRAW A SWORD TO START YOUR BACKHAND

To hit a strong backhand, you must rotate your upper body fully on the forward swing in order to put power into the shot and get your weight moving forward. To do that, imagine that you are pulling a sword out of its scabbard as you start your forward swing. Draw the racquet forward smoothly and turn your lead shoulder around. That way, your upper body will turn and your weight will start to move forward.

—*Mike Ratcliff*

TUCK IN YOUR ELBOW FOR A CONTROLLED BACKHAND

If your backhands are erratic, you may be hitting the ball too far away from your body. You can reduce that tendency by using a more compact backswing with your arm flexed and your elbow closer to your body. To check that your elbow is only two or three inches from your body, practice your backswing with a tennis ball tucked under your arm. If the ball falls out during the backswing you are straightening your arm too much. With your elbow tucked and your arm flexed on your backswing, your forward swing will be closer to your body so that you'll hit with more power and control.

—*Ben Foster*

KEEP YOUR BACK TO THE WALL FOR BETTER BACKHANDS

Many players have weak backhands because they flail at the ball with roundhouse strokes rather than swinging on a line toward the target. If that's your problem, imagine that you are standing with your back to a wall and are hitting the ball along a line parallel to that wall. Swing without hitting your make-believe wall with your racquet hand. That will compel you to take the racquet back no further than necessary, will prevent you from opening your shoulders too soon and will make you bring the racquet forward on a smooth path using your upper body, shoulders and arm. The result will be solidly hit, accurate backhands.

—*Andy Brandi*

73

LET YOUR SHOULDER POINT THE WAY TO POWER ON YOUR BACKHAND

On the backhand stroke, the body can impede a proper, full backswing which, in turn, puts a limit on how much power you can get into the stroke. You can lengthen your backswing and thereby increase your power simply by rotating your shoulders when taking your racquet back. Turn your body until the front shoulder points toward the contact point. You'll ensure a longer backswing and a more powerful backhand.

—*Rick Tavolacci*

75

WATCH THE BALL UNTIL YOU HEAR IT HIT

Having problems timing your hits? Try watching the ball until you hear it hit the racquet strings. Many players think that they have watched the ball all the way to impact but, in fact, they often take their eyes off it 15 to 20 inches away from contact. The result is a poorly hit shot. So watch the ball until you hear it strike the strings and you'll usually hit the ball solidly and accurately.   —*Doug Elgin*

SLOW YOUR SWING FOR GROUND STROKE POWER

Many beginning players swing too hard at the ball when hitting ground strokes. These wild swings often result in off-center hits with poor direction and a lack of power. Try slowing down your swing so that you hit cleanly through the ball. A smooth swing will help you hit the ball in the center of your racquet, produce a more powerful shot and help you avoid potential elbow strain. A slower, smoother swing will also be a more relaxed swing and, as a result, you'll have a more consistent stroke.

—*Flip LoGuidice*

79

KEEP YOUR OTHER ARM AT YOUR SIDE FOR BETTER BACKHANDS

Do you tend to spray your backhands all over the court? The problem may have nothing to do with your racquet swing. Surprising as it may seem, the blame may lie with your non-racquet arm. If you wave that arm around too much, you can force your body to open (rotate toward the net) before it should. And that will probably cause you to pull the ball wide or short. The solution is to keep your other arm at your side as you swing. That will compel you to remain sideways to the net through most of the swing. The result should be better control and direction. You can even put your other hand in your pocket until you have the habit of keeping your other arm at your side.

—Dave Kozlowski

SWING AT THOSE BACKHANDS WITH A FRISBEE TOSS

The arm motion for a backhand is almost exactly like that for a Frisbee toss. To throw a Frisbee, you should stand sideways to the target, draw your arm back close to your body, swing forward with your arm straight and release the Frisbee in front of your body. Your knees stay bent and your body rotates as the throw is made. If you are a proficient Frisbee thrower, you'll also have a long follow-through to help you get the proper direction. Try the uncoiling action of the Frisbee throw on your backhand and you'll find that it will help you keep your elbow close to your body (putting less strain on your arm) and will help put your racquet out in front where it belongs for a clean, well-timed stroke.

—*Dave Engleberg*

83

PLAY TUG-OF-WAR ON YOUR BACKHAND

If your backhand lacks power, the chances are that you are not putting your weight into the shot. One way to correct that problem is to imagine that you are involved in a tug-of-war and that your racquet handle is the rope which you're pulling from behind you. As you pull, you'll lean forward, pushing your weight off your back foot and into the stroke. This action will also help you to keep your elbow in and straight so that you hit through the ball rather than slap at it with a whippy motion. Put your weight into your backhand as though you were pulling in a tug-of-war and you'll put extra zip into your shots.   —*Rick Halpine*

THROW YOUR RACQUET TO AIM YOUR BACKHAND

If you have problems controlling the direction of your backhand shots, it may help if you imagine that you are throwing your racquet after the departing ball. Once you've hit it, follow through in the direction you'd like the ball to go. Think of throwing your racquet along that line. But don't actually let go, of course! The throwing action will point your arm and racquet to the spot you want the ball to go and you'll see it follow the line right to that spot. Don't freeze your motion after the throw, however. Let the racquet slow down naturally until you reach the end of your complete follow-through. Remember to simulate a throwing action just after impact and you'll soon have an accurate backhand.

—*Steve Greenberg*

IS YOUR BACKHAND FOR THE BIRDS?

If your backhand seems jerky, check to see if you're flapping your free hand. Should your hand fly up in the air as you make the stroke, it will cause you to pull up your entire body and the stroke will lose its fluidity. Try a few practice shots to see if your hand flaps aimlessly. If so, make a point of keeping your free hand low in a balanced position behind your body. That spare hand isn't for flapping, it's for helping your balance. Get rid of the flap and you'll restore smoothness to your stroke. —*Doug MacCurdy*

USE YOUR OTHER ARM LIKE A TIGHTROPE WALKER

Just as a tightrope walker uses both arms to maintain balance, a tennis player should use the non-racquet arm as a counterbalance. For example, on a forehand drive, extend your free arm toward the ball as you take your racquet back. As you begin moving your racquet forward, the other arm should then swing around at the same speed in the same direction to help you keep your balance throughout the stroke. You can also use your non-racquet arm for balance when you're at the net and when you're moving to hit a shot.

—*Lee Draisin*

91

KEEP YOUR WEIGHT OUT IN FRONT

If your backhand shots lack control, you may be putting too much weight on your heels as you follow through. Most players have a natural tendency to straighten their legs and throw their heads back as they complete a stroke. But that's wrong. Your weight should be on the front foot as you hit the ball and follow through. The way to achieve that is to keep your head down and keep your knees bent. Keeping your head down will automatically put the weight where it's needed—on the front foot. —*Hugh Curtler*

FREEZE WHEN YOU FINISH YOUR STROKE

Are you having trouble with your follow-through? The next time you are out practicing, stop your motion as you complete your stroke. You'll probably find that you have only a partial follow-through, and that's why you're not getting the proper direction on your shots. When you freeze your backhand or forehand, the follow-through should be as far out in front as possible with the racquet head up in the air. If you are stopping too soon, you'll have to extend the follow-through. Even when you play, you can still freeze momentarily to check on your follow-through action. —*Frank B. Walker*

HIT AND RUN ON THE COURT

Don't just stand around admiring your shot after you've hit the ball—get moving! As soon as you complete your stroke, start running. It is a rare shot in tennis that shouldn't be followed up by some fast footwork. Usually, you'll need to run back into position in the center of the court if you're at the baseline or to cover an angled return if you are at the net. Or you may want to run up to the net to follow an approach shot or move back to cover an expected attacking shot. Whatever the situation, don't just stand there. Move!

—*Ben Foster*

SERVE

BOUNCE THE BALL BEFORE YOU SERVE

If you do not already bounce the ball once or twice before you serve, you should start doing it. The bounce helps you build concentration for the serve by changing the focus from the last point played—a horizontal action—to the service toss and swing—a vertical motion. Bounce the ball approximately at the point where it would land if it were tossed correctly and fell without being hit. That will force you to get your weight onto your front foot for a proper start of the smooth shifts of body weight that will give you a powerful service. —*Mary P. Johnson*

SPREAD YOUR FEET FOR SERVICE POWER

If your service lacks consistency and power, you may be standing with your feet too close together. If your feet are not apart, you'll have a tendency to dip at the knees, which will result in a jerky and inconsistent motion. You'll also be unable to put your weight into the serve for maximum power. The cure is to stand with your feet spread slightly wider than your shoulders—or about a racquet's length apart. With your feet spread, your serve will be more fluid since you'll be able to rock back to start the motion and then transfer your weight forward to put power into the shot. —*Jim Burns*

TOE THE LINE FOR BETTER SERVES

Having trouble placing your serves? Check the position of your feet as you prepare to serve. An imaginary line crossing the tips of the toes of both your shoes should point along the intended line of flight of the ball. Keep your feet about shoulder width apart and check their position each time you serve. Make sure that the line across the toes is pointing to your target in the service box. —*Susan Riebel*

TAKE AIM BEFORE YOU FIRE YOUR SERVE

No part of the service is more difficult to master than the toss. But you can develop the necessary consistency in your toss if you follow this routine. Before starting your toss, hold the ball and your racquet in front of you and then look right over them into the service court; your head, your arms and the target should now be all in line. When you lift your arm for the toss, keep it in this line. The correct toss for a flat or spin serve should place the ball approximately six inches to a foot in front of your hitting arm. If the toss does not line up in front of your hitting arm, catch it and try again.

—*Ben Foster*

RELEASE THE BALL AT THE TOP OF YOUR REACH

Many players have difficulty with their serves because they do not contact the ball at the same place each time. This variation in hitting is largely due to the irregularity of the toss. Toss the ball to the same position and height each time and you'll find that you will get a more consistent serve. The secret of an accurate ball toss is to release the ball at the very top of your reach. Hold the ball with your fingertips and, when your arm is fully extended, release the ball by gently opening your fingers. If you wait to let go of the ball at the top of your reach, you'll develop consistency in your toss. And that will give you a more consistently accurate serve. —*Chuck Morrison*

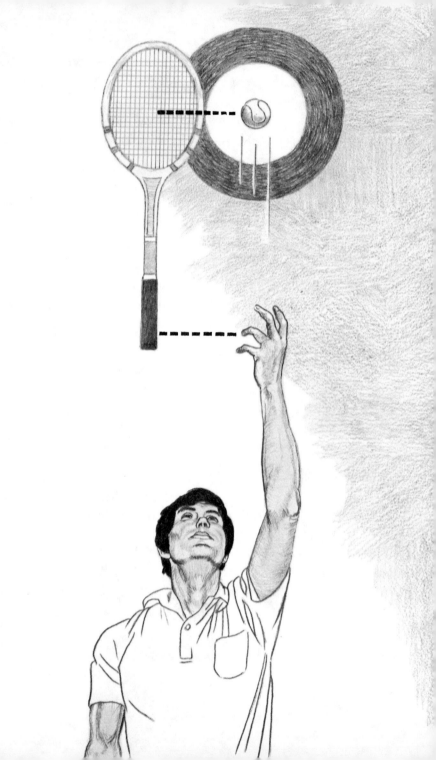

PERFECT YOUR BALLTOSS

At almost any level of tennis, the reason for a poor serve can often be traced to a faulty tossing technique. If the ball goes to different spots each time, it is impossible to develop a consistent serve.

Practice, of course, is required to correct the problem. And it is usually best, especially for beginners, to get away from the court for that practice so that concentration focuses only on the toss itself and not on where the ball is being hit.

I suggest standing sideways about an arm's length away from a wall. Practice tossing the ball up parallel to the wall to a height level with the very top of the racquet when it is held up with the arm fully outstretched. Keep at it until the ball is thrown to the same place every time. It will all pay off back on the court.   —*John Brownlow*

REACH FOR THE SKY WHEN RELEASING THE BALL

If you have a weak serve that frequently goes into the net, the root of the trouble is probably a cramped service motion. The odds are you're not lifting the ball high enough in the air before you hit it. The way to overcome the problem is to keep your ball hand rising after you've released the ball. As you watch the ball ascend, you should also see your ball hand reaching for the sky just before you tuck it down next to your body to get it out of the way of the racquet. Reaching for the sky will help you place the ball higher and, thus, correct that cramped service motion.   —*Denny Lewis*

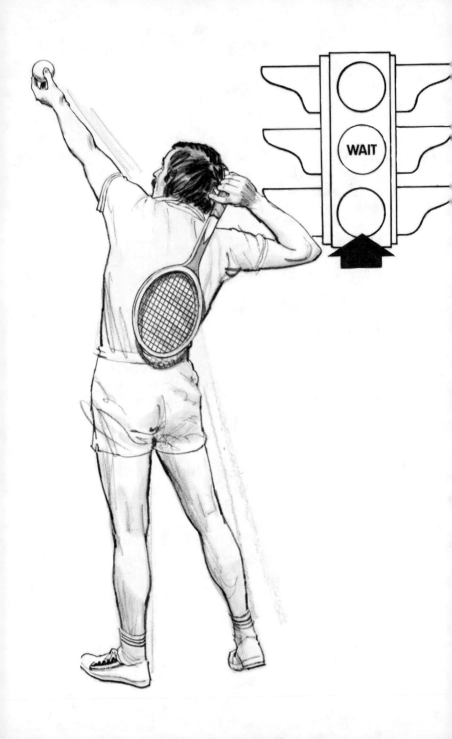

DELAY YOUR TOSS FOR A FULL BACK-SCRATCHING MOTION

If you are not getting the racquet head down behind your back in the back-scratching position as you should when you serve, the thing to do is release the ball a little later. By delaying your toss, you'll give your serving arm time to get the racquet back properly and then you'll be able to bring the racquet up sharply for a powerful serve. I recommend that you delay your ball toss until your racquet has gone behind your head. You can then release the ball, complete the back-scratching swing and, finally, bring the racquet up sharply to hit the serve.

—*Juan Rios*

115

SCRATCH YOUR BACK FOR A POWERFUL SERVE

If your serve seems to lack power and you have trouble timing the hit, you may not be taking your racquet back far enough. Drop the racquet head down behind your back before you swing forward to hit the ball. If you get your racquet in what's known as the back-scratching position, you'll be able to accelerate the head for a powerful hit. And back-scratching will stop you from bringing your shoulder around too early, which causes a loss of control.
—*Silas Everett*

ANCHOR YOUR FRONT FOOT WHEN YOU SERVE

To put any real power in your service, you must transfer your weight forward as you make contact with the ball. A reliable way to do that is to remember to keep your front foot anchored to the court as you serve. That way, your front foot can receive the weight of your body as it is transferred forward during the serve. With your front foot anchored, you can lift your back foot and swing it forward as your weight moves. That will also help get you moving if you plan to charge the net. Keep your front foot anchored, though, until after you've hit the ball.

—*Ben Foster*

POINT YOUR RACQUET TO THE SKY FOR A POWER SERVE

To get maximum power from your serve without injuring your shoulder or arm, remember to take your racquet well back and drop the head until the butt end of the handle is pointing to the sky. When it's in that position, your racquet will be in the proper back-scratching position and your wrist will be cocked for the start of the forward swing. That way, you'll be able to get a big swing and a healthy wrist snap as you hit the ball. So pointing your racquet handle to the sky will help you put extra power in your serve. —*Rick Halpine*

121

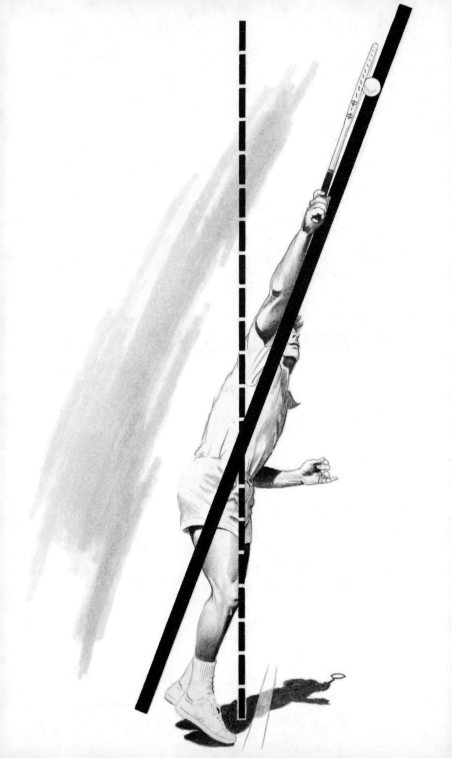

LEAN ON YOUR SERVE FOR MORE POWER

If your serve lacks real oomph, the reason may be that you're not putting your weight into it properly. To do that, push off from your back foot as you bring the racquet up on the serve so that at contact you are leaning into the court. As the ball is hit, you should be almost falling into the court with your body stretched out in a straight line from your ankles to the tip of your racquet. Don't bend at the waist because that won't put any body weight into the shot. Lean forward with your body fully extended as you hit the ball.
—*Paul M. Nemecek*

MEASURE YOUR CONTACT POINT TO IMPROVE YOUR SERVE

Whenever your serve becomes erratic, check to be sure that you are lifting the ball to the proper contact point. To find out where that is, simply swing your racquet up to the place where you normally hit the ball. You should be reaching up with your body stretched and your arm fully extended. Look at the middle of your racquet strings. That's where the ball should be when you hit it. Keep a mental picture of that contact point and release the ball so that it reaches that height.

—*Rick Tavolacci*

HIT THE BALL WHEN IT STOPS

If you have mastered the art of throwing the ball to the proper height for the serve, try and hit the ball at the peak of its flight. At its peak, the ball will stop momentarily before it begins to drop. You'll find that it's much easier to hit the ball in the center of your racquet when the ball is not moving. Don't hit a moving ball unless you have no choice.
—*Dennis J. Konicki*

SNAP YOUR WRIST LIKE A PITCHER WHEN YOU SERVE

Just before you hit the ball on your serve, you should snap your wrist forward as a pitcher would when throwing a baseball. The wrist snap will give your serve extra zip and help put spin on the ball. As you snap your wrist, you can rotate your palm slightly to help you aim the ball. It will go in the direction that the palm is pointing. For maximum power, continue the snap through the contact with the ball and into the follow-through. If you have trouble getting the feel of the wrist snap, try throwing a ball a few times before you serve.   —*Raymond Yost*

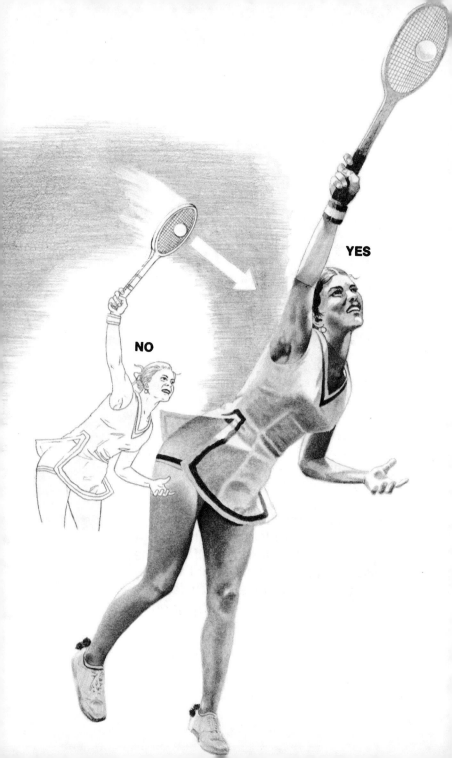

NO

YES

LOOK UP SO YOUR SERVE WON'T GO DOWN

Do many of your serves thud harm-
lessly against the net? If they do, the
reason probably is that you're dropping your head as you meet the ball. It
means that you can't watch the ball,
that your body bends prematurely at
the waist, that your wrist snaps too
soon and that you're hitting off balance. So be sure to keep your head up
and your eyes on the ball when you
serve. You'll get more accuracy and
power because you'll be hitting the
ball with a straight arm and a fully
extended body.   —*Gregg Kail*

THROW YOUR RACQUET FOR A DEEPER SERVE

If you are having trouble getting your serve over the net, here's something to try in practice that should help. Throw your racquet over, instead. It's best to use an old one if you can, and to avoid doing it when there are other people on the court. You'll probably find that the racquet will hit the ground in front of the net on your first try, indicating that you are either pulling your head or the racquet down—or both. Throw the racquet up and out, and you'll soon find that it will sail over the net. Now, use the same motion with your normal serve and you'll have an easy motion that will send the ball consistently deep.   —*Sean Sloane*

FOLLOW THROUGH FOR A FORCEFUL SERVE

You'll have a potent serve only if you use a full swing with a complete follow-through that carries the racquet sweeping out toward your opponent's court and down past your body on the side opposite your hitting arm. The racquet should end behind you. Try to complete the service swing with your racquet pointing at the fence behind you. This full swing will put the force of the whole arm and upper body into the serve. It also brings the wrist into play to put pace, spin and kick on the ball.

—*Ben Foster*

ALWAYS PLAY NETTED SERVES

How many times have you found yourself bored by an opponent who seems to hit all of his first serves into the net? Of course, when his serve finally does go in, you may be caught off guard and muff the return.

Why not compete against the netted serve? Imagine that you are actually going to play the return. Get your racquet back as quickly as you can after the ball leaves the server's racquet and get into position to hit the ball as if it were going to come through the net. This practice on netted serves will speed up your reaction time and quicken your reflexes to keep you alert when the serve does come in.

—*Dave Kozlowski*

137

HOP TO GET READY TO RETURN SERVES

When you're returning serve, hop lightly the moment the ball leaves the server's racquet to start your body turn for either a forehand or a backhand. By hopping in the air, you'll force your body to move, your racquet will start its backswing and you'll be on your toes when you land. The result will be an early start on the return and your body will be poised to make the stroke. But don't jump high in the air; a slight hop is all you need to get moving for your safe return. —*Edward Fuller*

VOLLEY

VOLLEY WITH YOUR BACK TO THE WALL

Fast volleying at the net calls for short, punchy strokes with little or no backswing. Take too long a backswing and you'll miss the shot completely. To shorten your backswing, imagine that you are standing with your back to a wall whenever you are inside the service line. The imaginary wall will stop you from taking your racquet farther back than your shoulder, thus forcing you to adopt a punching motion for your volleys. Swing back only as far as the wall and punch out in front of you for deeper and more accurate volleys.

—*Hugh Curtler*

AIM AT THE CENTER OF YOUR DOUBLES TARGET

When you are playing doubles, you should aim most of your shots at the center of your target—that is, down the middle of the court (except on return of serve). By directing the ball at the center, you give your opponents less chance to pass you with an angled shot and you'll also net fewer balls since the net is lower in the center. On top of that, a down-the-center shot can sometimes confuse the opposition as both partners try to hit the same ball. Aim for the center and the percentages will be on your side.   —*Henry Majkut*

CROSS OVER FOR HARD-TO-REACH VOLLEYS

If you are having trouble getting to those wide volleys, check your footwork. Chances are that you're stepping out with your right foot (if you're a right-hander) for those wide forehand volleys. That wrong step limits your reach quite severely. Next time, cross over with your left foot and you'll find that you can not only reach farther but you can easily bend down for those tricky low volleys. Practice that pivot and left-foot step and it will soon become standard procedure for your net play. Swift footwork at the net comes with the one-step crossover.

—*Chet Murphy*

ON LOW VOLLEYS, KEEP YOUR RACQUET HEAD HIGH

When you're in the forecourt, the hardest balls to volley are those that descend below the top of the net. Many players make the mistake of dropping the racquet head and scooping the ball back over the net; that only presents the opponent with a rising ball that can be put away easily. So it's vital on low volleys to keep the racquet head above the level of the wrist and just below the flight of the ball on the forward swing. You've got to bend sharply at the knees to do that. But with the racquet head high, you'll find that you can swing through the ball and send it skimming low over the net. Instead of a nice, fat setup to pounce on, your opponent will have a tough shot to contend with.   —*Jean Prevost*

GET OUT IN FRONT OF YOUR VOLLEYS

To hit an effective volley at the net, play the ball in front of your body, not to the side. Hold your racquet firmly in front of you and, as the ball approaches, step forward toward the net so as to bring your racquet into the line of the ball's flight. That way you'll cut off the volley as close to the net as possible, which usually gives you a higher ball to play and always gives you better angles down into your opponent's court. —*Ben Foster*

USE A KARATE CHOP ON YOUR HIGH BACKHAND VOLLEYS

The high backhand volley is a difficult shot because you have to chop, or slice, the ball to bring it down inside your opponent's court. To help you develop the proper slicing action, try hitting the ball with an action similar to a karate chop. The motion of your hand should be the same as it would be on a karate chop. Bring the bottom edge forward and down with a rapid slicing action as your racquet head approaches the ball. Done correctly, this karate chop volley will produce a crisp shot with a solid punch to it and enough spin for the control you need.

—*Ben Foster*

KNEEL ON YOUR REAR KNEE FOR LOW VOLLEYS

The key to hitting a good, crisp low volley is to get down to the ball. However, if you simply bend forward at the waist, the chances are that you'll bend your racquet face forward, too, causing the ball to go into the net. So on low volleys, you must bend your legs — enough so that your rear knee is almost touching the ground. That way, your upper body will be more upright and, as a result, you'll be able to hit the ball up and over the net. And, of course, your eyes will be closer to the line of flight of the ball which means you can watch it more easily.

—*Richard W. Fernan Jr.*

GET DOWN LIKE A SPRINTER FOR THOSE LOW VOLLEYS

Low volleys and half volleys are difficult shots at best, but you'll make them even more difficult if you bend only at the waist and drop the head of your racquet to meet the ball. You'll have much more success with these shots if you bend your knees as well as your back. In some cases, in fact, your knees should be bent so far that your back knee is nearly on the court. In this position, you'll be crouched something like a sprinter in his starting blocks. But this stance will permit you to get under the volley while keeping the racquet head up.   —Ben Foster

PAW YOUR VOLLEYS LIKE A CAT

Have you ever watched a cat reach out to paw at a passing insect? Your volley motion should duplicate the cat's quick, short movement from the shoulder. The racquet will move only a short distance but it must be accelerating quite rapidly at contact to give control and depth to your volleys. So the next time you are crouched at the net preparing to volley, imagine that you are a cat and the ball is a passing butterfly. Reach out and paw the ball as it comes over the net.

—Dan Campbell

SQUEEZE YOUR GRIP AS YOU HIT FOR A SOLID VOLLEY

If your volleys are erratic, you may have a floppy grip that allows the racquet to wobble in your hand as you hit the ball. Try giving your racquet handle a quick, firm squeeze as if you were trying to squeeze an orange — at ball contact. The firmer grip will keep your racquet steady in your hand and, as a result, produce more accurate and effective volleys. But don't grip the racquet tightly throughout the stroke because your hand and arm muscles will become fatigued. Just squeeze firmly as you hit the ball.   —*Charles Tyrrell*

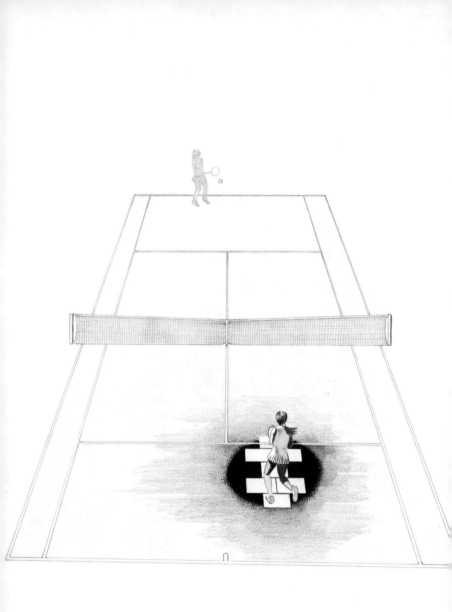

HOPSCOTCH TO YOUR FIRST VOLLEY

Remember how you used to play hopscotch as a child? You'd run, pause and then jump to either side. Do the same things as you head toward the net following your serve. Pause momentarily as your opponent returns your serve, decide where the return is going and then move diagonally to that side, just as you would if you were playing hopscotch. Imagine that the hopscotch layout is on the court just in front of the service box and you'll be close to the best position for your first volley.   —*Peter Allen*

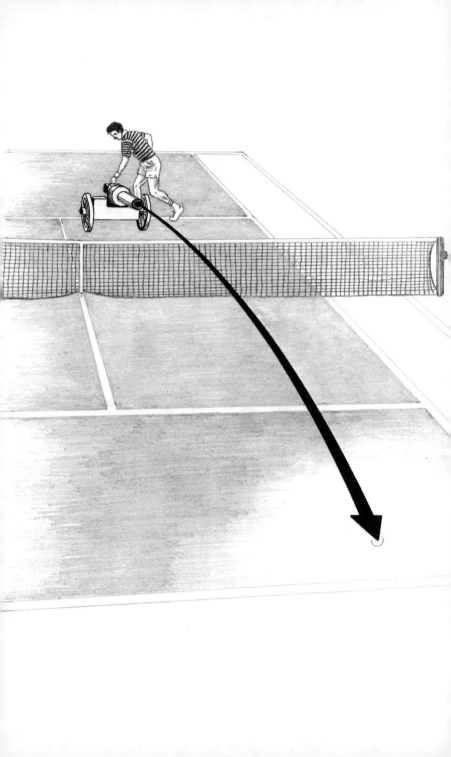

ATTACK WITH YOUR FIRST VOLLEYS

Once you've got yourself placed properly for volleying, don't waste the opportunity. You're in an attacking position — so attack with your heavy artillery.

The first volley should land within three to four feet of your opponent's baseline and, if possible, in the open court. Now, press your advantage by moving further toward the net several steps in the direction of your volley.

If your first volley does not penetrate, does not make your opponent move for the ball and does not keep him off balance, he'll take your volley and perhaps do terrible things to your confidence — like pull off a devastating passing shot. So make the first volley work for you. —*Chuck Morrison*

TWO DRILLS FOR SHARPER VOLLEYS

How many times have you seen a player who is faced with an easy volley slam the ball into the net or out of the court? You can help prepare yourself for easy touch shots by practicing the volley at the net with a partner. Try to keep the ball off the ground and in play as long as possible until someone misses. Then you can take turns feeding balls from the baseline so the person at the net can practice placements to different parts of the court. These two drills should help sharpen up your volleys quickly. —*Henry Majkut*

PRACTICE FIRST VOLLEYS FROM THE SERVICE LINE

Most players like to volley from a position about five to eight feet from the net. At that distance, few balls can drop to your shoelaces. The odds are, though, that you'll have to hit your first volley before that while you're still on your way up to the net. Usually, you'll be right around the service line. So during your next practice session, why not practice volleys from that point? To hit solid volleys from the service line, get down low and keep your wrist very firm. Practice a few volleys like that and notice how your serve and volley game will improve. —Doug MacCurdy

LOB

WHEN IN TROUBLE, LOB

I can remember an old-time radio program that used to introduce each episode with, "When in trouble, call the sheriff." In tennis, that phrase should be changed to, "When in trouble, hit the lob." What can you do when an opponent runs you deep and to a corner of the court? Lob, lob, lob!

Lobs can be hit offensively and defensively. The defensive one is not designed to fool the opponent; it is designed to give you time to recover and regain court position. To gain enough time, be sure to hit the ball very high and deep (think of the sheriff and aim for a star). Too many players fail to resort to the lob when it is the only way you can keep the ball away from the opponent long enough to recover time and position. After all, he can't hit it when it's 40 feet in the air.

—*Chuck Morrison*

RETREAT LIKE AN OUTFIELDER FOR DEEP LOBS

To retrieve a lob that is going to bounce near the baseline, don't merely back-pedal facing the net. You won't be able to get back fast enough. Instead, like an outfielder chasing down a deep fly ball, turn your body and feet toward the back fence, watch the ball over your shoulder and run. By turning tail this way, you'll move faster and cover more ground. And, of course, your upper body will already be turned sideways and your racquet will be back, meaning that you will be ready to swing at the ball as soon as it reaches you. But remember to keep watching the ball over your shoulder. *—Ben Foster*

CHECK YOUR LOB FOR HEIGHT AND RANGE

A good lob is actually a cross between two shots: a direct drive over the net and a ball hit straight up in the air. A lob should obviously get the kind of depth you'd expect from a drive and it will need height to clear your opponent at the net. So if you're having difficulty in getting the feel for a lob, try two swings: one a line drive and one a vertical shot. Then try a shot between the two. With a little practice, you'll not only get the feel for the shot but you'll also get the right height and range just like the Navy gunner who fires off test rounds. —*Dave Kozlowski*

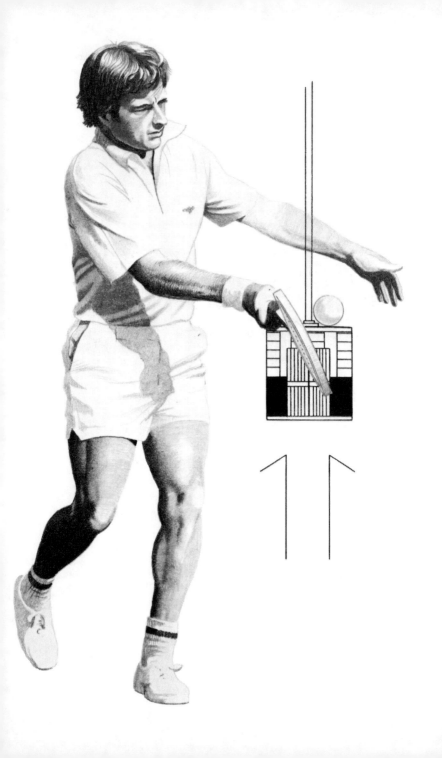

PUT YOUR LOBS ON AN ELEVATOR WHEN YOU FOLLOW THROUGH

To hit higher, deeper lobs, keep your racquet on the ball longer and follow through more fully. Think of your racquet as an elevator. The ball should get on at the bottom floor with contact about waist high. Lift your racquet through contact and keep on lifting it after contact until your arm is fully extended upward. Your follow-through will make you feel that the ball stayed on the racquet much longer. Use a smooth upward motion like an elevator and your lobs will go higher and deeper.   —James Burns

OVERHEAD

BE PREPARED FOR THE SMASH

Get your racquet up and back when you prepare for an overhead smash. If you let your racquet dangle by your side, you'll take too large and too late a swing. To be ready for the smash, have your racquet cocked behind your ear on your racquet side. The racquet head should be down your back in the "back-scratching position." With your hitting arm in this position, your swing will be shorter and more controlled. You'll experience no loss in power and a great gain in accuracy.—*Ben Foster*

TRACK THOSE OVERHEADS

Weekend tennis players blow the overhead smash more than possibly any other shot. But there are times when you should smash, especially close to the net. Be sure to position the ball in front of you, reach up with your free arm to judge—i.e., track—the descent, and get your racquet behind your ear. Don't wind up as you do for the serve, and don't let your zeal for a spectacular smash prevent your executing the stroke properly.—*Raymond Schuessler*

EVERYONE AFRAID OF OVERHEADS SAY EYE!

Hitting a solid no-nonsense overhead provides one of the bigger thrills of tennis. Confidence in your ability to handle this stroke adds a whole new dimension to your game. If you avoid overheads because they cause you trouble — perhaps embarrassment — chances are you're making the most common overhead error, lowering your head before you contact the ball.

Players often make this mistake because they unconsciously glance at their target area instead of keeping their eyes on the approaching ball. As you move into position semi-sideways to the ball with your racquet back, keep your head up and eyes on the ball until you make contact just in front of your forehead, with your arms fully extended. *—Tom Hammang*

187

ATTACK YOUR OVERHEADS FROM BEHIND

Do most of your overheads crash pointlessly into the net? If they do, it's probably because you hit down on the ball too much and, thus, create too sharp an angle for the shot to clear the net adequately. To prevent your smashes from nosediving into the net, attack the ball from behind as though you intend to drive it horizontally. Your wrist snap and follow-through will be enough to bring the ball down into your opponent's court. By attacking the ball from behind, you'll hit deep smashes that will go over—not into—the net.

—*Dan Campbell*

189

REACH UP TO MEET THE BALL ON YOUR OVERHEAD

When hitting an overhead, reach up to hit the descending ball. That way, the contact point will be slightly in front of your body and as high as you can reach so you'll hit the ball with a full swing for a powerful shot. If you wait too long to hit your overheads, you'll contact the ball with a cramped swing which will reduce your power and accuracy. So reach up to meet the oncoming ball and you'll find that you'll soon stop mishitting your overheads.

—Fernando Pinho